KALE

The Leafy Green Powerhouse for Vibrant Health and Culinary Delights (2023 Guide for Beginners)

Sydney Daniel

Learn about Kale.

Kale is a hardy vegetable that is accessible all year, although it is at its peak from mid-September to late-February. It is possible.

It might be difficult to prepare since it is rough and fibrous. The following are some of my tried-and-true methods for picking and prepping vegetables to make cooking them a breeze every time.

Kale Variety

Curly kale, red kale, and Tuscan/dinosaur/lacinato/cavolo Nero kale are the most popular forms of kale seen in stores.

Curly and red kale are coarse and tightly coiled in appearance. The former is light to brilliant green in hue, whilst the latter is a deeper shade of green with purple stems.

When eaten fresh, this kale has a strong peppery taste and may be harsh and toothsome. Its substantial texture and folds allow sauces to cling to it, making it an excellent option for meals that need longer cooking periods, such as stews and casseroles.

The Tuscan kale, also known as dinosaur, lacinato, or cavolo Nero kale, is longer and has spear-like leaves.

The leaves are flatter and do not wrinkle like curly or red kale. Instead, they have a pebbled, lumpy appearance and a rich, earthy taste. They break down considerably more easily than their curly cousin and are more suited for eating raw or for recipes that need less cooking time, like as stir-fries and pastas.

Kale, curly

Kale in red

 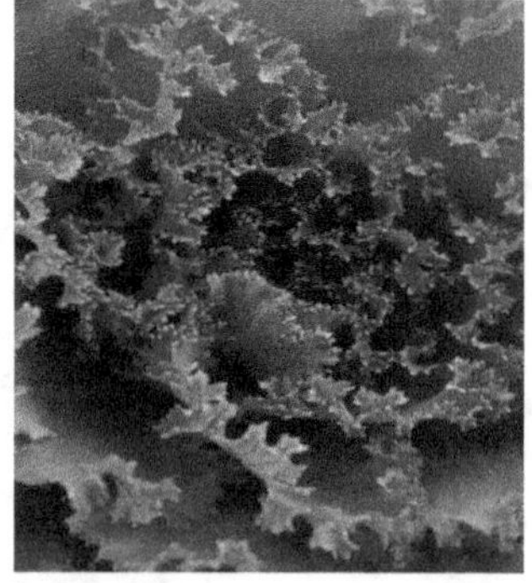

Kale from the Tuscan region

 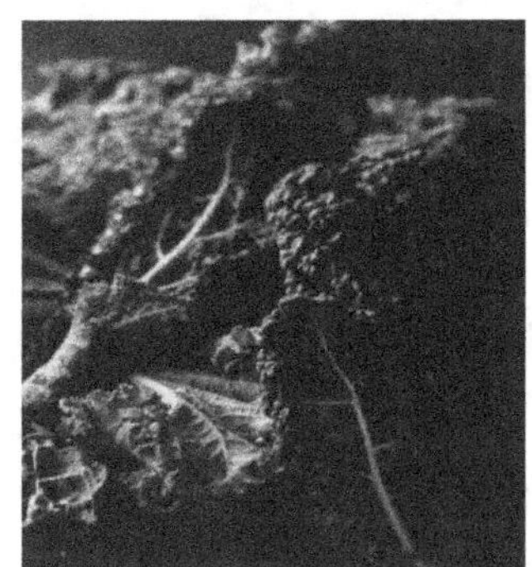

How to Select Kale

Choose brightly coloured kale leaves. The longer the veggie is on the shelf, the bitterer it will taste. Avoid kale with yellow leaves, which indicate that it has lost nutrients and has been stored in the refrigerator for too long.

Choose smaller heads of kale for kale that has a milder taste and is more delicate. The fresher and smaller the leaves, the less bitter it is likely to be. As a result, if you plan to eat it raw, consider smaller kale leaves that are simpler to digest.

To store it, put unwashed kale leaves in a plastic bag in the refrigerator. Keep in mind that the longer kale sits in the fridge, the more probable it may acquire a bitter taste. Consume it within 2-3 days after buying it.

Organic kale is a wonderful option for avoiding pesticides.

How to Cook Kale

To prepare kale, thoroughly wash it in cold water to remove dirt and grit as well as any pesticides. Separate the leaves from the woody centre rib using a sharp knife. The thicker and stiffer centre stalk of the leaves should be removed since it does not tenderize as much as the leaves when cooked.

If you're going to consume the kale raw, cut it into thin ribbons or smaller pieces. In a large mixing basin, combine the kale and a dash of sea salt. Scrunch the kale briefly with clean hands until it turns aromatic and dark green.

Drizzle a prepared dressing over the greens and toss to cover well. Allow the kale to rest for at least 10 minutes before serving to allow the dressing to break down the rough greens.

Kale salads are ideally made a day ahead of time to allow the greens to soften and become more digestible. They may be stored for up to 2-3 days without becoming wet or wilting.

If you're planning to cook the kale, coarsely slice the leaves into bite-sized pieces. Take care not to overcook it, since this will turn it bitter and unpleasant to eat.

The most frequent ways to prepare kale are to boil or steam it.

If you want to steam it, put it in a steamer basket in a saucepan of boiling water for 5 minutes, or until soft. To boil it, place the kale in a saucepan of salted boiling water and cook for 4-5 minutes, or until the leaves are brilliant green but softer. To halt the cooking process, drain and rinse with cold water.

Recipes for Breakfast

Ingredients for Kale and Bacon Egg Tart

Servings: 4

1 (8 ½ ounce) store-bought frozen puff pastry sheet, defrosted

2 large eggs

1 cup half-and-half cream

¼ teaspoon salt

⅛ teaspoon pepper

⅛ teaspoon nutmeg

½ cup bacon, chopped

1 cup red onions, sliced

8 cups baby kale

Preparation

1. Preheat the oven to 425 degrees Fahrenheit.

2. Fit a 9-inch tart pan with a detachable bottom with the puff pastry sheet. Cover all of the edges and sides of the pan, then cut off any extra dough. Prick holes all over the pastry with a fork.

3. Bake for 10 minutes, or until golden brown. If the pastry has risen, carefully flatten it with the back of a fork. Reduce the oven temperature to 400°F.

4. Prepare the pie filling while the crust is baking. Whisk together the eggs and cream in a medium mixing bowl, seasoning with salt, pepper, and nutmeg. Set it aside for now.

5. Fry the bacon in a medium pan over medium heat until it begins to crisp. Place the bacon on a dish lined with paper towels to drain any excess oil.

6. Wipe out all except 1 tablespoon of bacon grease from the pan with a clean piece of paper towel. Over medium-high heat, sauté the onions until soft and lightly browned. Cook for 2-3 minutes, covered, with the kale. Remove the cover and continue to simmer for another 2-3 minutes, or until the spinach is thoroughly wilted.

7. Arrange the veggies on the crust and top with the bacon. Pour the egg mixture in. Stir the ingredients lightly to ensure equitable distribution.

8. Bake for 25 minutes, or until the filling is completely set. Remove from the oven and set aside for 10 minutes to cool.

Nutritional Information (235 g per serving)

- Calories 587
- Fats 43 g
- Carbohydrates 36 g
- Protein 15 g
- Sodium 568 mg

Salad with Strawberries and Kale with Crunchy Granola

Servings: 2

Ingredients

8 ounces kale, stems and ribs removed, roughly chopped

½ pound strawberries, hulled and sliced

5 medium radishes, thinly sliced

2 ounces goat cheese

1 cup of granola

Dressing:

3 tablespoons olive oil

2 tablespoons lemon juice (about 1 small lemon)

1 tablespoon smooth Dijon mustard

1 ½ teaspoons honey

Salt and pepper, to taste

Preparation

1. In a large mixing bowl, knead the kale with a pinch of salt for approximately 1–2 minutes, or until the kale darkens and softens somewhat.

2. In a small mixing bowl, combine the dressing ingredients. Pour the dressing over the greens. Toss the kale with the dressing until evenly covered.

3. Toss in the strawberries and radishes. Sprinkle the oats on top of the salad and crumble the goat cheese on top.

4. Set aside the salad for 15 minutes before serving.

Nutritional Information (644 g per serving)

- Calories 1097
- Fats 84 g
- Carbohydrates 75 g
- Protein 21 g
- Sodium 198 mg

Pie with chestnuts, kale, and mushrooms

Servings: 6

Ingredients

2 tablespoons unsalted butter

1 onion, finely chopped

3 ½ ounces celery, finely chopped

2 cloves garlic, finely chopped

1 ½ ounces dried porcini mushrooms, soaked for 30 minutes in

boiled water

4 cups chestnut mushrooms, cut into chunks

10 fresh sage leaves

3 ½ ounces cooked chestnuts, roughly chopped

¼ cup all-purpose flour

1 ½ cups whole milk

Salt and pepper, to taste

6 cups kale, stems and ribs removed, roughly chopped

14 ounces store-bought puff pastry

1 large egg, beaten

Preparation

1. Preheat the oven to 400 degrees Fahrenheit.

2. Melt the butter in a large pan over medium heat. Cook for 10 minutes, covered, with the onion and celery. Remove the cover, add the garlic, and simmer for 5 minutes more.

3. Drain and roughly slice the rehydrated mushrooms.

Stir-fry the mushrooms, sage, and chestnuts in the skillet for 5 minutes.

4. Mix the flour into the veggies. Drizzle the milk into the skillet slowly while swirling constantly until the mixture thickens. Season with salt and pepper to taste.

5. Heat a big pot of water to boiling. Cook for 3 minutes, or until the kale softens but keeps its brilliant colours. To end the cooking, drain the water and rinse the kale under cold water.

Transfer the kale to a clean tea towel and pat dry to remove any extra moisture. Combine the greens and mushroom mixture in a mixing bowl. Pour it into a 12-quart baking dish.

6. Roll out and trim the store-bought puff pastry until it is slightly larger than the pan. Cut a vent in the centre of the pastry with a knife.

7. Brush the top of the pastry generously with egg wash. Bake the dough for 25 minutes, or until golden brown and the filling is steaming.

Nutritional Information (278 g per serving)

- Calories 521
- Fats 33 g
- Carbohydrates 47 g
- Protein 12 g
- Sodium 233 mg

Kale, Brussels Sprouts and Potato Hash

Servings: 4

Ingredients

4 pounds Yukon gold potatoes, or any waxy potatoes, cut into ¾-inch

chunks

3 tablespoons vegetable oil, divided

Salt and pepper, to taste

12 medium Brussels sprouts, finely sliced

2 cups tightly packed chopped kale leaves

1 small onion, finely sliced

1 teaspoon hot sauce

2 tablespoons minced fresh parsley leaves

2 eggs

Preparation

1. Preheat the oven to 450 degrees Fahrenheit.

2. Cover the potatoes with cold salted water in a medium saucepan.

Over high heat, bring the water to a boil. Reduce the heat to medium and continue to cook the potatoes for another 5 minutes, or until they are slightly tender. Drain and put aside the potatoes.

3. In a large oven-safe skillet, heat 2 tablespoons of oil. Cook for 5 minutes, or until the potatoes begin to colour. Transfer to a clean platter and season with salt and pepper.

4. Heat another tablespoon of oil in the same skillet. Sauté the Brussels sprouts and kale for 3 minutes, or until they begin to wilt. Continue cooking the onions until the veggies begin to crisp up, around 5-8 minutes.

5. Toss the veggies with half of the parsley and the spicy sauce. Season with salt and pepper, then add the potatoes.

6. In the vegetable mixture, make two wells. Fill each well with an egg. Bake for 5-8 minutes, or until the egg whites are set. Sprinkle the remaining parsley over the top of the dish.

Serve right away.

Nutritional Facts (593 g per one serving)

- Calories 602
- Fats 24 g
- Carbohydrates 88 g
- Protein 15 g
- Sodium 112.5 mg

Frittata with Kale and Goat's Cheese

Servings: 4

Ingredients

1 tablespoon olive oil

2 finely sliced red onions

½ pound curly kale leaves

1 tablespoon water

2 tablespoons balsamic vinegar

8 big beaten eggs

1 cup crumbled hard goat's cheese

Preparation

1. Preheat the oven to 400 degrees Fahrenheit.

2. Heat the oil in a medium skillet or oven-safe frying pan over medium heat. Cook for 10-15 minutes, or until the onions are softened and browned.

3. Cook for approximately 5 minutes, or until the kale has wilted, with the water. Cook for about a minute after adding the balsamic vinegar.

4. Pour the eggs into the pan and quickly mix to ensure that all of the ingredients are spread equally. Turn the heat down to medium-low. Allow the eggs to simmer for another 5 minutes, or until they are almost set. At this stage, do not disturb the eggs.

5. Sprinkle the goat's cheese on top of the frittata. Bake for 10-15 minutes, or until the eggs are set and the frittata is golden brown.

Nutritional Information (328 g per serving)

- Calories 316
- Fats 21 g
- Carbohydrates 11 g
- Protein 21 g
- Sodium 804 mg

Recipes for Appetizers and Snacks

Citrus Cumin Salt Kale Chips

Servings: 6

Ingredients

1 teaspoon cumin seeds

1 teaspoon flakes sea salt

1 pound cleaned and dried kale

Rapeseed oil drizzle

1 lemon's zest

Preparation

1. Preheat the oven to 320 degrees Fahrenheit. Using parchment paper, line a baking sheet.

2. To create the cumin salt, roast the cumin seeds in a small pan over medium heat until aromatic and slightly brown. In a spice grinder or pestle and mortar, combine the roasted cumin seeds and sea salt flakes. Blend until the mixture is finely ground.

3. Separate the kale leaves from the stems and stalks, leaving big sections intact. Coat the leaves with oil and arrange them in a single layer on the prepared baking sheet. 6 minutes in the oven. Allow them to cool after removing them from the oven. As it cools, the kale will crisp up.

4. Season with cumin, salt, and lemon zest to taste.

Nutritional Information (18 g per serving)

- Calories 8
- Fats 0 g
- Carbohydrates 2 g
- Protein 1 g
- Sodium 394 mg

Spread with Kale and Feta

Servings: 2

Ingredients

2 cups curly kale leaves

½ cup low-fat soft cheese

⅔ cup feta

½ teaspoon capers

1 teaspoon fresh dill, roughly chopped

1 tablespoon olive oil

Season with salt and pepper to taste.

Preparation

1. Fill a medium saucepan halfway with water and bring to a boil.

Cook for 5–8 minutes, or until the kale has wilted. Remove it from the steamer and place it on a platter to cool.

2. In a food processor, combine the kale, cheeses, capers, dill, and olive oil until smooth. Season with salt and pepper to taste.

Nutritional Information (134 g per serving)

- Calories 320
- Fats 27 g
- Carbohydrates 8 g
- Protein 13 g
- Sodium 697 mg

Hand Pies with Kale and Sausage

Servings: 8

Ingredients

2 ½ cups all-purpose flour

1 cup unsalted butter, cut into small pieces

1 ½ teaspoons salt

½ cup cold water

1 tablespoon extra-virgin olive oil

10 ounces sweet Italian sausage, casings removed

1 medium onion, diced

1 Granny Smith apple, peeled and diced

1 pound kale, stems and ribs removed, roughly chopped

¼ cup golden raisins

Season with salt and pepper to taste.

As a pastry wash, use whole milk.

Preparation

1. Combine the flour, butter, and salt in a food processor. Pulse the components together until they resemble a coarse meal. While the machine is working, slowly drip in the cold water until the dough begins to come together. Remove the dough from the machine and shape it into a disc. Refrigerate the

dough for at least 30 minutes after wrapping it in plastic wrap.

2. Heat the oil in a large skillet over medium-high heat. Cook for 6 minutes, or until the sausages are browned. While the meat is cooking, split it up with a wooden spoon. Remove any extra fat.

3. Cook for approximately 5 minutes, or until the onion is transparent. Toss in the apple, kale, and raisins and simmer for 5 minutes, or until the kale wilts. Season with salt and pepper to taste.

Place it in a clean basin and put aside.

4. Preheat the oven to 400 degrees Fahrenheit. Two baking sheets should be lined with parchment paper.

5. On a lightly floured board, roll out the dough to 18-inch thickness.

Cut out 8 circles using a 6- or 7-inch cookie cutter. Divide the kale mixture into 8 equal parts and place one in the middle of each piece of dough. Fold the dough in half to make a half moon shape.

Using a fork, crimp the edges of each pie. Place the pies on the baking pans that have been prepared. Make a tiny vent in each pie and brush with milk.

6. Bake for 25-30 minutes, or until golden brown. Allow to cool gently on a wire rack before serving hot.

Nutritional Information (157 g per serving)

- Calories 522
- Fats 36 g
- Carbohydrates 39 g
- Protein 10 g
- Sodium 705 mg

Wonton with chicken and kale

Servings: 30 wontons

Ingredients

1 cup kale leaves, thinly sliced

¼ cup yellow onion, finely chopped

½ pound ground chicken thigh meat

½ cup water chestnuts, finely chopped

2 tablespoons green onion, thinly sliced

Season with salt and pepper to taste.

30 wrappers for wontons

Canola oil is used for frying.

Preparation

1. In a medium microwave-safe dish, place the kale. Microwave on high for 3–5 minutes, or until the kale has wilted, covered with plastic wrap.

2. Season the onion, ground chicken, water chestnuts, softened kale, and green onion in a large mixing bowl with salt and pepper.

3. Place one spoonful of filling in the middle of each wonton wrapper. Apply some water to the wrapper's edges. Fold the wrapper diagonally to make a triangle. To seal the wonton, lightly push down the edges. Rep till you have 30 wontons.

4. Heat the canola oil in a heavy-bottom skillet over high heat until it reaches 350°F. Fry 3–5 wontons at a time in heated oil till golden brown, rotating

periodically. Drain excess oil by placing them on a tray lined with paper towels.

5. Serve with your preferred dipping sauce.

Nutritional information (20 g per serving)

- Calories 36
- Fats 1 g
- Carbohydrates 5 g
- Protein 2 g
- Sodium 51 mg

Crostini with Kale and Parmesan

Servings: 8

Ingredients

1 baguette, sliced ½-inch thick diagonally

3 tbsp extra-virgin olive oil (divided)

Season with salt and pepper to taste.

4 minced garlic cloves

2 pounds kale, removing stems and ribs, chopped into strips

1 cup of water

2 tablespoons freshly squeezed lemon juice

1 little wedge Parmesan

Preparation

1. Preheat the oven to 400 degrees Fahrenheit.

2. Lay the bread pieces out on a baking pan. Season with salt and pepper and brush with 1 tablespoon olive oil.

Bake for 8 to 10 minutes, or until gently browned.

Take the tray out of the oven.

3. Heat 2 tablespoons oil in a large pan over medium heat.

Sauté the garlic for 30 seconds, or until aromatic. Stir in the greens for approximately 5 minutes, seasoning with salt and pepper. Reduce the heat to medium, add the water, and cook for approximately 10 minutes with the lid on.

Remove the cover and continue to cook for another 3-5 minutes, or until the majority of the liquid has evaporated.

4. Combine the greens and lemon juice in a mixing bowl.

5. Arrange the cooked kale on top of each bread piece. Finish with a few shaved pieces of Parmesan.

Nutritional Information (98 g per serving)

- Calories 163
- Fats 10 g
- Carbohydrates 10 g
- Protein 9 g
- Sodium 264 mg

Balls of Sweet Potato and Kale

Servings: 10-12 balls

Ingredients

2 medium sweet potatoes, peeled and cut into ½-inch pieces

2 tbsp unsweetened coconut milk

1 cup finely chopped kale leaves

1 medium coarsely chopped shallot

1 teaspoon cumin powder

½ teaspoon granulated garlic

½ teaspoon sea salt

Preparation

1. Preheat the oven to 400 degrees Fahrenheit. Using parchment paper, line a baking sheet.

2. To cook the sweet potatoes, bring an inch of water to a boil in a medium saucepan. Place the sweet potatoes in a steamer basket and steam for 10–15 minutes, or until cooked. Allow it to cool in a big mixing basin before handling.

3. Mash the sweet potato with a potato masher while pouring in the coconut milk until fully combined and smooth. Combine the kale, shallot, cumin, garlic, and salt in a mixing bowl.

4. Form 10-12 balls with a spoon and slightly damp palms. Place them on the baking sheet that has been prepared. Bake for 20 to 25 minutes, or until the balls are firm. Allow them to cool for 5 minutes before digging in to firm them somewhat.

Nutritional information (35 g per per serving based on ten balls)

- Calories 36
- Fats 1 g
- Carbohydrates 6 g
- Protein 1 g
- Sodium 132 mg

Dip with Kale and Hummus

Servings: 1

Ingredients

1 clove garlic

2 oz. grated Parmesan

1-pound fresh kale leaves

1 can chickpeas (14 oz.) drained and rinsed

1 teaspoon of lemon juice

6 tbsp extra virgin olive oil

Season with salt and pepper to taste.

Preparation

1. In a food processor, combine all of the ingredients. Blend until it achieves the desired consistency, such as a smooth puree. If the dip is too thick, add more olive oil to thin it up.

Nutritional Information (410 g per serving)

- Calories 1318
- Fats 104 g
- Carbs 67 g
- Protein 35 g
- Sodium 1654 mg

Bites of Kale and Quinoa

Servings: 24

Ingredients

2 ½ cups cooked quinoa

4 large eggs, beaten

½ teaspoon sea salt

1 finely chopped tiny onion

½ cup feta crumble

1 minced garlic clove

1 cup finely chopped kale leaves

½

cup edamame shelled

¾ breadcrumbs

Unsalted butter (for frying)

Preparation

1. Preheat the oven to 375 degrees Fahrenheit. To prevent the muffins from sticking, thoroughly butter 24 mini-muffin pans.

2. Combine the quinoa, eggs, salt, onion, feta, garlic, kale, edamame, and breadcrumbs in a large mixing basin. Allow the mixture to stand for 5 minutes to allow the breadcrumbs to absorb the liquid.

3. Divide the mixture equally among the muffin cups. Bake for 25-30 minutes, or until the eggs are completely set.

4. Remove the muffins from the oven and set aside for 5 minutes. To loosen the muffins, run a knife over the sides. Remove the quinoa bites from the pan and place them on a wire rack to cool fully.

Nutritional Information (40 g per serving)

- Calories 61
- Fats 2 g
- Carbs 7 g
- Protein 3 g

- Sodium 116 mg

Mini Salad Cups with Kale

Servings: 24

Ingredients

1 cup all-purpose flour for the crust

½

teaspoon of salt

6 tbsp vegetable shortening (cut into tiny cubes)

2 to 4 tbsp cold water

1 egg

1 teaspoon milk

Salad:

2 cups finely chopped kale leaves

1 granulated sugar cup

½

tsp Dijon mustard

½

teaspoon of salt

3 tablespoons white wine vinegar

½

cup of extra virgin olive oil

1 ½

tablespoons poppy seeds

1 pomegranate seed cup

Preparation

1. Preheat the oven to 350 degrees Fahrenheit. Coat 24 mini-muffin pans with cooking spray.

2. In a food processor, combine the flour, salt, and shortening until the mixture resembles a coarse meal. Drizzle in 2 teaspoons of cold water while the machine is running until all of the components mix to make dough. If required, add extra water. Flatten the dough into a disc, cover it in plastic wrap, and place it in the freezer for 15 minutes.

3. Roll the dough out to 18-inch thickness on a lightly floured board.

Cut circles from the dough using a 3-inch cookie cutter. Fill the mini-muffin pan holes with the dough, making sure it covers the bottom and edges of the cup.

4. In a small mixing dish, combine the egg and milk combination. Brush the mixture on top of the shells. Cook for 15 minutes, or until golden brown. Remove the cups from the pan and set them aside to cool fully.

5. In a large mixing bowl, combine the sugar, mustard, salt, vinegar, oil, and poppy seeds. Add the greens and massage them with the dressing. Allow for a 10-minute rest before serving.

6. To serve, spoon the kale salad into each cup. Finish with the pomegranate seeds.

Nutritional Information 29 g (per serving)

- Calories 103
- Fats 8 g
- Carbs 7 g
- Protein 1 g
- Sodium 150 mg

Bites of Cheesy Kale

Servings: 14

Ingredients

2 pounds of kale leaves

½ cup thawed frozen peas

½ cup shredded mozzarella

¼ cup Parmesan cheese, grated

¼ cup cornmeal

1 egg

½

tsp onion powder

½

teaspoon of salt

Preparation

1. Preheat the oven to 375 degrees Fahrenheit. Using parchment paper, line a baking sheet.

2. Start a kettle of water to boil. Cook for 3-5 minutes, or until the kale is soft but still has a brilliant green colour. To stop the cooking, drain and rinse the kale under cold water. Squeeze out any extra water from the kale. Place the kale in a food processor.

3. Finely grind the kale with the peas, cheese, cornmeal, egg, onion powder, and salt.

4. Using a tablespoon, divide the mixture into bite-sized balls and place them on the baking sheet that has been prepared. Bake for 20 minutes or until firm to the touch.

5. Serve hot

Nutritional Information (29 g per serving)

- Calories 35
- Fats 2 g
- Carbs 4 g

- Protein 2 g
- Sodium 124 mg

Recipes for Soups

Soup with Kale and White Beans

Servings: 8

Ingredients

2 tablespoons of olive oil

4 garlic cloves, chopped

2 celery stalks, cut

1 big sliced onion

Season with salt and pepper to taste.

2 washed 15-ounce cannellini beans

1 cup of orzo

1 pound chopped kale, stems, and ribs removed

2 tbsp fresh rosemary, chopped

8 c. water

Calories 35

½

cup of shaved Parmesan cheese

1 tablespoon freshly squeezed lemon juice

Preparation

1. Heat the oil in a large soup pot over medium-high heat.
2. Cook the garlic, celery, and onion until soft, approximately 4-6 minutes. Season with salt and pepper to taste.
3. Combine the beans, orzo, kale, rosemary, and water in a mixing bowl. Bring the water to a boil. Reduce the heat to low and cook for 4-5 minutes, or until the pasta is done and the kale is soft.
4. Add the lemon juice and mix well. Serve immediately, topped with a heavy sprinkling of Parmesan.

Nutritional Information (174 g per serving)

- Calories 257
- Fats 13 g
- Carbs 28 g
- Protein 10 g
- Sodium 367 mg

Lentil and Kale Soup

Servings: 6

Ingredients

1 tablespoon extra virgin olive oil

4 leeks, cut into 14-inch sections

1 can (28 oz.) whole tomatoes, drained

6 c. water

1 big peeled and chopped into bite-sized chunks sweet potato

1 pound chopped kale, stems, and ribs removed

½

cup cooked brown lentils

1 tablespoon thyme, fresh

Season with salt and pepper to taste.

Preparation

1. Heat the oil in a large, deep pan or Dutch oven over medium heat.

2. Sauté the leeks for 3-4 minutes, or until softened. Put the tomatoes in the pot. Break up the tomatoes with the back of a spoon and let them bubble for 5 minutes.

3. Fill the skillet halfway with water and bring it to a boil. Season with salt and pepper and stir in the sweet potato, kale, lentils, and thyme. Continue to cook for 25-30 minutes, or until the lentils are cooked.

4. Serve right away

Nutritional Information (300 g per serving)

- Calories 268
- Fats 9 g
- Carbs 40 g
- Protein 13 g
- Sodium 188 mg

Soup with Roasted Butternut Squash and Kale

Servings: 6

Ingredients

2 pounds peeled, deseeded, and cut into bite-sized pieces of squash

2 sprigs of fresh rosemary

3 tbsp olive oil (divided)

Season with salt and pepper to taste.

1 pound orzo pasta

1 sliced onion

2 smashed garlic cloves

1 finely chopped red chili

6 cups vegetable stock

3 cups coarsely sliced curly kale leaves

1 lemon juice

Grated Parmesan is an optional garnish.

Preparation

1. Preheat the oven to 400 degrees Fahrenheit.

2. Arrange the squash in a roasting pan. Toss with the rosemary sprigs and 2 tablespoons of the oil; season to taste with salt and pepper. Cook for 30 minutes, or until the squash is soft. Remove from the oven and set aside to cool.

3. Boil a large kettle of salted water. Cook the orzo according to package directions. Set it aside to drain.

4. Heat 1 tablespoon oil in a large pan over medium heat.

Cook the onion for approximately 10 minutes, or until it softens. Stir in the garlic and red Chile for 30 seconds. Bring the broth to a boil in a saucepan. Cover and cook for approximately 5 minutes, or until the veggies have wilted. Combine the orzo, squash, and lemon juice; season with salt and pepper to taste.

5. Garnish with a heavy sprinkling of grated Parmesan and serve immediately.

Nutritional Information (506 g per serving)

- Calories 403
- Fats 21 g

- Carbs 50 g
- Protein 7 g
- Sodium 757 mg

Soup with Ham, Kale, and Pasta

Servings: 4

Ingredients

1 big thinly sliced onion

1 tablespoon extra virgin olive oil

2 smashed garlic cloves

2 ½

cup packed kale leaves, chopped

6 cups chicken broth (low sodium)

8 oz. rotini or any chosen short pasta

1 cup deli ham, shredded

1 tablespoon freshly squeezed lemon juice

Season with salt and pepper to taste.

Preparation

1. Heat the oil in a large skillet over medium heat. Cook for approximately 10 minutes, or until the onion has softened. Sauté for 30 seconds after adding the garlic. Pour in the broth and toss in the greens. Bring

the liquid to a boil, then lower it to medium-low heat. Simmer for 10 minutes, covered.

2. Heat a saucepan of salted water. Cook the rotini according to package directions. Drain and combine with the soup.

3. Stir in the ham and lemon juice, and season to taste with salt and pepper.

4. Dig in!

Nutritional Information (552 g per serving)

- Calories 434
- Fats 6 g
- Carbs 71 g
- Protein 24 g
- Sodium 1235 mg

Soup with Kale and Sweet Potato

Servings: 4

Ingredients

1 tablespoon extra virgin olive oil

1 yellow onion, chopped 1 shallot, chopped 2 peeled and chopped carrots

2 pounds sweet potatoes, peeled and sliced into bite-sized portions 1 stalk celery, chopped

1 bay leaf 2 sprigs fresh thyme

4 c. water

Season with salt and pepper to taste.

Kale 1 pound

Preparation

1. Heat the oil in a big, deep skillet over medium heat. Cook for 5 minutes, or until the onions are transparent.

2. Combine the sweet potatoes, bay leaf, and thyme in a mixing bowl. Bring the water to a boil in a saucepan. Reduce the heat to low, cover, and let the veggies cook for approximately 30 minutes, or until soft and tender.

3. Take out the bay leaf and the thyme sprigs. Puree the soup with an immersion blender until smooth.

4. Add the greens and season with salt and pepper to taste. Cook for another 10 minutes, covered, to allow the kale to wilt.

Nutritional Information (614 g per serving)

- Calories 303
- Fats 4 g
- Carbs 63 g
- Protein 6 g

- Sodium 186 mg

Recipes for Salads

Salad with apples, kale, and pancetta

Serving: 4

Ingredients

⅓ cup virgin olive oil

4 ounces diced pancetta

1 small head shredded radicchio 8 ounces kale,
stems and ribs removed, leaves sliced into bite-sized
pieces

2 apples, thinly cut into matchsticks

¾ cup pecans

Dressing:

¼ cup white wine vinegar

¼ cup maple syrup

To taste, a pinch of salt and pepper

Preparation

1. Heat the oil in a small skillet over medium heat and
cook the pancetta until crispy. Remove it to a paper
towel to absorb any excess oil.

2. To create the dressing, combine the vinegar and maple syrup in a mixing bowl; season with salt and pepper.

3. Toss the dressing with the radicchio, kale, and apple in a large mixing basin. Allow the mixture to settle for 5 minutes to soften the greens.

4. Plate and serve the salad. Finish with the pancetta and pecans.

Nutritional Information (259 g per serving)

- Calories 870
- Fats 83 g
- Carbs 31 g
- Protein 7 g
- Sodium 202 mg

Salad with lentils, carrots, and kale

Servings: 4

Ingredients

1 green lentil cup

3 cups vegetable broth (low sodium)

3 peeled carrots, sliced into 14-inch circles

1 onion (cut in half)

1 clove

one bay leaf

Season with salt and pepper to taste.

1 pound kale, stems and ribs removed, ribboned

1 minced garlic clove

Dressing:

2 tablespoons of olive oil

2 tablespoon sherry vinegar

1 tablespoon Dijon mustard

Preparation

1. Combine the lentils and vegetable broth in a large pot and bring it to a boil.

2. To the saucepan, add the carrots, onion, clove, bay leaf, and a pinch of salt. Bring the broth to a boil, then lower it to low heat.

Simmer the lentils for 25 minutes, or until soft.

3. Remove any extra liquid from the lentils and veggies and place them in a clean dish. Remove the clove and bay leaf.

Season with salt and pepper to taste.

4. Heat the oil in a medium skillet over medium heat. Fry the greens for 3-4 minutes before adding the garlic and cooking for another minute.

Season with salt and pepper to taste. Mix in the greens with the lentils.

5. Whisk together the olive oil, vinegar, and mustard to create the dressing. Season with salt and pepper to taste. Toss the lentils with the dressing until fully incorporated.

6. Serve immediately or preserve in the refrigerator for up to 2 days.

Nutritional Information (424 g per serving)

- Calories 443
- Fats 22 g
- Carbs 49 g
- Protein 18 g
- Sodium 569 mg

Salad with Roasted Squash and Kale

Servings: 4

Ingredients

1 pound butternut squash

2 tbsp of olive oil

three tbsp brown sugar

½ teaspoon of salt

⅓ teaspoon black pepper

1 pound finely sliced kale

1 peeled and julienned cucumber

¼ cup finely sliced red onion

Dressing:

2 tsp soy sauce (low sodium)

1 teaspoon lime juice

2 tbsp. sesame oil

1 granulated sugar teaspoon

2 tbsp. smooth peanut butter

2 teaspoons grated fresh ginger

1 teaspoon water

Preparation

1. Preheat the oven to 400 degrees Fahrenheit.

2. Peel and remove the butternut squash seeds. Cut it into bits and place them on a baking pan. Drizzle with olive oil and season with sugar, salt, and pepper. Bake for 25 minutes, or until the butternut squash is soft with a fork.

Allow it to cool after removing it from the oven.

3. In the meanwhile, make the dressing. Combine the soy sauce, lime juice, sesame oil, granulated sugar, peanut butter, ginger, and water in a mixing bowl.

4. In a large mixing basin, combine the butternut squash, kale, cucumber, and onion. Once the veggies have been coated with the dressing, they are ready to serve.

Nutritional Information (339 g per serving)

- Calories 529
- Fats 26 g
- Carbs 28 g
- Protein 9 g
- Sodium 812 mg

Slaw with Kale and Red Cabbage

Servings: 4

Ingredients

1 cup kale, shredded

2 cups red cabbage, shredded

1 peeled and julienned carrot

¼ cup fresh parsley, chopped

2 tbsp. red onion, diced

two tbsp sunflower seeds

two tbsp pumpkin seeds

2 tbsp of hemp seeds

Dressing:

1 tablespoon extra virgin olive oil

1 tbsp. Dijon mustard

1 tsp apple cider vinegar

Season with salt and pepper to taste.

Preparation

1. In a small mixing bowl, combine the olive oil, mustard, and vinegar. Season with salt and pepper to taste.

2. Combine the kale, cabbage, carrot, parsley, onion, and various seeds in a large mixing basin.

3. Pour the dressing into the dish and toss the veggies to coat.

Nutritional Information (86 g per serving)

- Calories 185
- Fats 17 g
- Carbs 7 g
- Protein 3 g
- Sodium 23 mg

Salad with Kale and Fennel

Servings: 4

Ingredients

7 oz. feta cheese cut into 1-inch-thick slices

½ teaspoon olive oil

1 lemon's zest

1 lemon juice

To taste, season with salt and black pepper.

3 cups kale (baby)

1 ½ cups shaved fennel

¾ cup pecorino

½ cup roasted pine nuts

Dressing

½ cup freshly squeezed lemon juice

8 oz. olive oil, extra-virgin

seasoned with salt and black pepper

Preparation

1. Preheat the oven to 400 degrees Fahrenheit. Using parchment paper, line a baking sheet.

2. Arrange the feta pieces on a baking sheet. Season with salt and pepper and drizzle with olive oil, lemon zest, and juice. Bake for 15 minutes or until golden brown on the outside. Allow cooling after removing from the oven.

3. In the meanwhile, mix all of the dressing ingredients in a small dish until well combined.

4. Combine the kale and shaved fennel in a large mixing basin.

Massage the dressing into the leaves and let aside for 10 minutes.

5. Garnish the salad with crumbled feta, grated pecorino, and pine nuts.

Nutritional Information (233 g per serving)

- Calories 846
- Fats 85 g
- Carbs 13 g
- Protein 14 g
- Sodium 403 mg

Salad with Kale, Edamame, and Avocado from Asia

Servings: 4

Ingredients

1 pound kale, stems and ribs removed, thinly sliced

1 cup snow peas, rough ends removed and diced

1 big peeled carrot sliced into thin ribbons

1 little deseeded and sliced red bell pepper

1 cup defrosted frozen edamame

1 pitted and sliced avocado into small bits

1 big, thinly sliced shallot

2 teaspoons chopped cilantro

2 teaspoons chopped basil

a pinch of sea salt

Dressing:

¼ cup olive oil for dressing

two tbsp rice vinegar

1 tablespoon ginger, finely grated

1 teaspoon of soy sauce

2 tbsp. lime juice

3 minced garlic cloves

Preparation

1. In a large mixing bowl, knead the kale with a pinch of salt for approximately 1-2 minutes, or until the kale darkens and softens somewhat.

2. Toss in the snow peas, carrot, bell pepper, edamame, avocado, shallot, cilantro, and basil.

3. In a separate small dish, whisk together the dressing ingredients.

4. Drizzle the dressing over the salad and mix well.

5. Serve immediately or store in the refrigerator for up to two days.

Nutritional Information (293 g per serving)

- Calories 325

- Fats 24 g
- Carbs 24 g
- Protein 11 g
- Sodium 283 mg

Salad with Kale, Bacon, and Dates with Poached Egg

Servings: 4

Ingredients

6 slices sliced low-sodium bacon

2 tbsp. white wine vinegar

four huge eggs

1 pound kale, stems and ribs removed, ribboned

2 teaspoons finely sliced red onion

½ cups pitted and chopped Medjool dates

2 tablespoons chopped flat-leaf parsley

Dressing:

1 tablespoon coarse Dijon mustard

2 tbsp of mayonnaise

1 tablespoon vinegar (white wine)

½ teaspoon of honey

2 tbsp of olive oil

¼ teaspoon black pepper

Preparation

1. Cook the bacon in a medium pan over medium-high heat for 5 minutes, or until crispy. Remove it from the skillet and place it on a dish lined with paper towels to drain the excess oil. When the bacon has cooled, cut it into bite-sized pieces.

2. Bring a small saucepan of white vinegar and water to a boil. Turn the heat down low. Swirl the water with a spoon to produce a whirlpool.

Place one egg in the centre of the whirlpool and poach it for 3-4 minutes, or until the egg whites have set.

With a slotted spoon, remove the poached egg and put it aside.

Repeat until all of the eggs are done.

3. Combine all of the dressing ingredients in a mixing bowl.

4. In a large mixing basin, combine the kale. Pour one-third of the dressing into the mixing bowl. For around 1-2 minutes, massage the dressing into the kale.

5. Toss the kale with the onion, dates, and parsley. Pour the remaining dressing over the veggies and toss to coat evenly.

6. To serve, scatter the chopped bacon over the salad and top with a poached egg.

Nutritional Information (262 g per serving)

- Calories 569
- Fats 48 g
- Carbs 21 g
- Protein 17 g
- Sodium 436 mg

Salad with Kale, Carrots, and Feta

Servings: 4

Ingredients

1 pound chopped kale, stems, and ribs removed

1 tablespoon extra virgin olive oil

½ red onion, diced 2 carrots, shredded

1 shredded zucchini

½ teaspoon of sea salt

¼ tsp black pepper

½ cup of water

¼ cup dried cranberries, currants, or raisins

1 cup crumbled feta

4 cooked brown rice bowls

Preparation

1. Warm the olive oil in a large pan over medium heat.

6 minutes later, the onion should be transparent.

Combine the carrots and zucchini with salt, pepper, and water.

Cook, covered, for 10-15 minutes, or until the kale has wilted.

2. Toss the veggies with the raisins and feta.

3. Serve with brown rice or spaghetti.

Nutritional Information (452 g per serving)

- Calories 496
- Fats 21 g
- Carbs 65 g
- Protein 16 g
- Sodium 560 mg

Salad with Kale and Brussels Sprouts, Sweet and Savory

Servings: 2

Ingredients

1-pound curly green kale, removing stems and ribs, coarsely sliced

½ fresh and raw Brussels sprouts

3 tbsp. roasted sliced almonds

¼ cup shaved Parmesan cheese

1 tsp sea salt

¼ cup tahini for dressing

2 tbsp. white wine vinegar

2 tbsp. white miso

2 tbsp. maple syrup

1 tsp red pepper flakes

¼ cup of water

Preparation

1. In a large mixing bowl, knead the kale with a pinch of salt for approximately 1–2 minutes, or until the kale darkens and softens somewhat.

2. Trim the dark ends of the Brussels sprouts and remove any wilted leaves. Thinly slice the sprouts. Combine them with the kale.

3. In a small mixing bowl, combine the dressing ingredients. If the dressing is too thick, add additional water to thin it down to the appropriate consistency.

4. Drizzle the dressing over the salad and mix well.

5. Garnish with a liberal dusting of almonds and Parmesan.

Nutritional Information (422 g per serving)

- Calories 490

- Fats 28 g
- Carbs 46 g
- Protein 25 g
- Sodium 586 mg

Nutritional Information (286 g per serving)

- Calories 439
- Fats 32 g
- Carbs 12 g
- Protein 26 g
- Sodium 426 mg

Recipes for Main Dishes

Stew with sausage, kale, and barley

Servings: 4

Ingredients

3 tablespoons olive oil, split

8 hot dogs

2 sliced white onions

2 peeled and sliced carrots

¼ cup pearl barley (rinsed in cold water)

4 ½ cups chicken broth

2 rosemary sprigs, finely chopped

1 ⅓ cup kale, stems and ribs removed, coarsely chopped salt and black pepper to taste

Preparation

1. Heat 2 tablespoons of oil in a large pan over medium heat.

Fry the sausages for 10-12 minutes, or until browned on both sides.

Place the sausages on a clean platter lined with a paper towel and put them aside.

2. In the same pan, heat another tablespoon of oil over medium-high heat. Cook until the onions and carrots are slightly soft, approximately 5 minutes. Mix in the barley until it is well covered with the liquids.

3. Pour the liquid and rosemary into the skillet. Season with salt and pepper to taste. Cook for 10 minutes, covered, over medium heat. Return the sausages to the pan and cook for another 20 minutes, or until the meat is thoroughly cooked through.

4. Stir in the kale and simmer for another 5-10 minutes, or until wilted.

5. Serve right away.

Nutritional Information (594 g per serving)

- Calories 989
- Fats 69 g
- Carbs 59 g
- Protein 35 g
- Sodium 2281 mg

Chinese Spicy Kale and Beef

Servings: 4

Ingredients

1 pound thinly sliced beef strips (filet mignon, flank steak, sirloin steak)

2 teaspoons grated fresh ginger

4 minced garlic cloves

¼ teaspoon smoked paprika 1 medium onion, grated

2 dried red peppers

¼ tsp coarse salt

1 tablespoon of olive oil

1 ½ pounds chopped kale, stems, and ribs removed

½ cup beef stock (low sodium)

The spice of black pepper

Preparation

1. Toss the beef with ginger, garlic, onion, paprika, chiles, and salt in a medium mixing bowl.

2. In a large skillet over medium-high heat, heat the oil. Fry the seasoned meat for 2-3 minutes, or until it is gently browned.

3. Stir in the greens and turn the heat down to medium-low. Cook for 3 minutes, cover, then uncover and stir for another minute, or until the kale is wilted and soft.

4. Pour the broth into the skillet and scrape the pan's bottom with a spatula. Cook for 1 minute to decrease.

5. Before serving, season with pepper.

Nutritional Information (348 g per serving)

- Calories 265
- Fats 8 g
- Carbs 19 g
- Protein 34 g
- Sodium 336 mg

Baked Pasta with Chicken and Kale

Servings: 6

Ingredients

¾ cup dry bowtie pasta

2 tbsp unsweetened butter

1 big sliced yellow onion

3 minced garlic cloves

1 ½ pounds chopped kale, stems, and ribs removed

2 cups cooked shredded chicken

6 cups ricotta (skimmed)

3 tbsp. lemon zest, grated

¾ cup parmesan cheese, grated

seasoned with salt & pepper

Preparation

1. Preheat the oven to 350 degrees Fahrenheit.

2. Bring a big saucepan of salted water to a boil over high heat. Cook the pasta according to the package directions. Set aside after draining.

3. Meanwhile, in a large pan over medium-high heat, melt the butter. Fry the onion for 3 minutes, or until softened. Cook for another minute after adding the garlic.

4. Add the kale and mix to combine. Cook, covered, for 5 minutes, or until the veggies are soft.

5. Toss the cooked pasta with greens, chicken, ricotta, lemon zest, and ½ cup Parmesan. Season with salt and pepper to taste.

6. Put the pasta mixture in a baking dish. Scatter the remaining cheese over the top of the spaghetti.

7. Bake the cheese for 30 minutes, or until golden brown and bubbling.

Nutritional Information (483 g per serving)

- Calories 767
- Fats 31 g
- Carbs 69 g
- Protein 56 g
- Sodium 531 mg

Stew with chicken, chickpeas, and kale tomatoes

Servings: 4

Ingredients

1-pound breadcrumbs

3 tbsp extra-virgin olive oil (divided)

4 skinless boneless chicken breasts

Season with salt and pepper to taste.

1 finely sliced shallot

1 minced garlic clove

1 tsp dried red chili flakes

1 tbsp. dried oregano

1 tablespoon thyme dried

1 can whole peeled tomatoes (28 oz.)

1 cup chicken stock (low sodium)

1 can chickpeas (14 oz.) drained and rinsed

2 cups stem and ribs removed from kale leaves cut into ribbons

Preparation

1. Toast the breadcrumbs in a large pan over medium heat for 2-3 minutes, or until golden brown. Place them in a basin and set them away.

2. Heat 2 tablespoons of oil in the same skillet over medium-high heat. Season the chicken breasts lightly with salt and pepper and lay them in the pan. Cook for 5-6 minutes on each side, or until golden brown. Place the chicken on a clean dish.

3. Melt another tablespoon of oil in a skillet over medium-high heat. Fry the shallot for 2 minutes. Cook for another minute, or until the garlic, Chile flakes, oregano, and thyme are aromatic.

4. To the pan, add the tomatoes with their sauce and the chicken stock. Break up the tomatoes into big bits with the back of a spoon. Bring the mixture to a simmer and set aside for 10 minutes to thicken.

5. Return the chicken to the pan and cook for 5 minutes more. Combine the chickpeas and greens in a mixing bowl. Cook for 5 minutes, covered, or until the kale has wilted.

6. Garnish with breadcrumbs, if desired.

Nutritional Information (646 g per serving)

- Calories 655
- Fats 21 g
- Carbs 43 g
- Protein 72 g
- Sodium 909 mg

Mexican Chicken, Potato, and Kale Casserole

Servings: 6

Ingredients

1 pound chicken thighs, bone-in, and skin-on

Season with salt and pepper to taste.

2 tbsp vegetable oil (divided)

1 little peeled and sliced onion

2 minced garlic cloves

1 teaspoon thyme dried

1 teaspoon cumin powder

½ teaspoon coriander powder

3 canned chipotles in adobo + 3 tablespoons adobo
sauce

1 can peeled plum tomatoes (28 oz)

6 cups curly kale, removing stems and ribs, coarsely
chopped

3 big peeled and thinly sliced russet potatoes

1 ¾ cup shredded mozzarella

Sour cream, avocado, chopped fresh cilantro leaves,
and lime wedges for garnish

Preparation

1. Preheat the oven to 400 degrees Fahrenheit. Line a
baking pan with aluminium foil.

2. Season the chicken on both sides well with salt
and pepper. Place the chicken in the preheated pan,
skin side up.

Bake for 20–30 minutes, or until the meat is well
cooked.

3. Take the chicken out of the oven and set it aside to
cool fully. Remove the skin from the meat and shred
it. Reduce the oven temperature to 375°F.

4. Make the sauce while the chicken is cooking. Heat
1 tablespoon of the oil in a large pan over medium–

high heat. Fry the onions for 5 minutes, or until they are transparent and tender.

Cook until the garlic, thyme, cumin, and coriander are aromatic. Combine the chipotles, adobo sauce, and tomatoes in a mixing bowl. Bring the sauce to a boil, then lower to low heat and continue to cook for 15 minutes. Allow it to cool somewhat before using an immersion blender to mix it. Season with salt and pepper to taste.

5. Clean the skillet and reheat the leftover oil. Cook the kale for 3 minutes, covered, over medium heat. Remove the cover and cook for another 2 minutes, or until the meat is soft.

6. To construct, spread ¾ cup of the sauce in the bottom of a 9x13 baking dish, followed by a layer of potato slices, half the kale, ½ cup of mozzarella, and half the shredded chicken. Repeat the layers, finishing with potato pieces and cheese. Bake for 30 minutes with the dish covered with foil. Remove the foil and bake for a further 15 minutes, or until the top is golden brown and bubbling.

7. Garnish with sour cream, avocado slices, cilantro, and lime wedges if desired.

Nutritional Information (462 g per serving)

- Calories 464
- Fats 22 g
- Carbs 44 g
- Protein 24 g
- Sodium 466 mg

Roll of Pork Loin with Mushrooms and Kale

Servings: 8

Ingredients

2-pound hunk of pork

3 tbsp extra virgin olive oil

10 minced white mushrooms

1 chopped shallot

½ tsp dried thyme

½tsp dried sage

½ tsp garlic powder

½ teaspoon black pepper, ground

¼ teaspoon of salt

¼ cup fresh parsley, chopped

2 cups chopped fresh kale, stems, and ribs removed

1 tablespoon Dijon mustard

Preparation

1. Preheat the oven to 350 degrees Fahrenheit.

2. Trim the pork loin of any superfluous fat. Cut the meat horizontally from the centre, parallel to the chopping block, until it can be folded open like a book.

Wrap the meat in plastic wrap and pound it with a meat mallet.

3. Heat 1 tablespoon oil in a large pan over medium heat.

Sauté the mushrooms, shallot, herbs, garlic powder, pepper, and salt until the liquid is almost gone. Allow the kale to wilt for approximately 5 minutes. Mix in the mustard with the veggies.

4. Spread the mushroom and kale mixture evenly over the pork loin, leaving a ½-inch border on both sides. Roll the pork loin lengthwise and knot it with kitchen twine away from you.

5. Heat 2 tablespoons of oil in a large pan over medium heat.

Place the roll in the pan and cook the meat until golden brown on both sides.

6. Put the meat in a 9x13 baking dish. Bake for 35-40 minutes, or until the meat is fully cooked through (165°F on a meat thermometer).

7. Remove the pan from the oven and set aside for at least 10 minutes to enable the meat to rest. Before slicing into the roll, remove the string.

Nutritional Information (158 g per serving)

- Calories 283
- Fats 19 g
- Carbs 2 g
- Protein 28 g
- Sodium 174 mg

Kale and pork Baked Gnocchi

Servings: 4

Ingredients

Gnocchi (one pound)

1 tablespoon extra virgin olive oil

2 cups ground extra-lean pork

2 grated zucchinis

1 teaspoon crushed fennel seeds

¼ teaspoon chili flakes

1 garlic clove, coarsely chopped

⅔ cup curly leaf kale stems and ribs removed, diced

1 pound cheese sauce

¼ cup fresh breadcrumbs 1 cup cherry tomatoes, halved

¼ cup shredded cheese

Preparation

1. Preheat the oven to 400 degrees Fahrenheit.

2. Bring a big saucepan of salted water to a boil over high heat. Cook the gnocchi according to the package directions. 1 cup of pasta water should be saved.

3. Heat the oil in a large skillet over medium heat. Cook the pork for 5 minutes, or until it is golden and crisp. Season with fennel seeds, chili flakes, and garlic before adding the shredded zucchini. Cook for another 2 minutes after adding the greens.

4. Combine the pork mixture, cheese sauce, gnocchi, tomatoes, and leftover pasta water in a mixing bowl.

5. Place the gnocchi-pork mixture in a baking tray. On top of the spaghetti, sprinkle the breadcrumbs and grated cheddar.

6. Bake the cheese for 15-20 minutes, or until golden brown.

Nutritional Information (483 g per serving)

- Calories 806
- Fats 50 g
- Carbs 55 g
- Protein 34 g
- Sodium 953 mg

Tacos with beef and kale

Servings: 4

Ingredients

1 tablespoon extra virgin olive oil

½ lb ground beef

2 carrots, grated 2 garlic cloves, chopped

½ teaspoon of sea salt

1 teaspoon of chili powder

1 teaspoon cumin powder

two tbsp tomato paste

1 cup of water

12 taco shells made with corn

2 cups of kale leaves, thinly sliced

1 cup grated cheddar

12 tablespoon salsas

Preparation

1. Preheat the oven to 300 degrees Fahrenheit.

2. Heat the oil in a large skillet over medium-high heat. Fry the meat, carrots, and garlic for about 4-5 minutes, or until the carrots soften. Remove any excess oil.

3. Add salt, chili powder, cumin, and tomato paste to taste. Stir everything well and heat for another minute. Pour in the water, reduce the heat, and cook for approximately 4-5 minutes, or until the meat is tender.

4. Heat the taco shells according to the package directions.

5. To assemble, put 2-3 tablespoons of meat into each shell, followed by a handful of greens and cheese. Finish with 1 teaspoon of salsa. Take a bite and enjoy!

Nutritional Information (201 g per serving)

- Calories 529
- Fats 35 g
- Carbs 32 g
- Protein 21 g
- Sodium 797 mg

Lamb and Kale Stew

Servings: 4

Ingredients

2 tablespoons melted butter

½ cup celery, diced 1 cup carrots, chopped 1 big onion, chopped

½ cup chopped red pepper 1 pound ground lamb

2 minced garlic cloves

½ teaspoon cumin powder

one bay leaf

1 can tomato paste (6 oz.)

3 cups chopped packed kale, stems, and ribs removed

2 cups chicken stock with minimal sodium

Season with salt and pepper to taste.

Preparation

1. Melt the butter in a large saucepan over medium heat. Fry the onion, celery, and carrots for 7 to 10 minutes, or until the veggies soften.

2. Stir in the ground lamb and red pepper until the meat is browned, approximately 5 minutes. Season with salt and pepper after adding the garlic, cumin, and bay leaf. Mix in the tomato paste and greens, and give everything a thorough stir.

3. Pour in the chicken stock and bring it to a boil. Reduce the heat to a low simmer, cover, and cook for 20-25 minutes.

4. Before serving, remove the bay leaf.

Nutritional Information (401 g per serving)

- Calories 460
- Fats 33 g
- Carbs 19 g
- Protein 23 g
- Sodium 598 mg

Tangy Mackerel and Kale Spaghetti

Servings: 4

Ingredients

2 tbsp extra-virgin olive oil (divided)

⅓ pound breadcrumbs

1 teaspoon chili powder

1 minced garlic clove

4 fillets of mackerel

4 quarts spaghetti

3 cups chopped kale leaves, stems, and ribs

1 lemon, zipped and juiced

2 tablespoons capers, washed and chopped

Season with salt and pepper to taste.

Preparation

1. In a large pan, heat half a tablespoon of the oil. Toast the breadcrumbs with the chili flakes and garlic for 4 minutes, or until golden brown and aromatic. Place the breadcrumbs on a clean dish.

2. Heat another half teaspoon of oil in the same skillet. Cook the mackerel skin-side down for 4-5 minutes. Cook for a further 3 minutes on the opposite side. Set the fish aside on a clean dish after flaking it with a fork.

3. Meanwhile, heat a large pot of salted water to a boil.

Cook the pasta according to the package directions. Add the kale to the saucepan in the final 4 minutes of cooking time.

Drain all except 2 tablespoons of the cooking liquid when the noodles have finished cooking and the kale has softened. Put the pasta and greens back in the pot.

4. Toss the pasta with the saved cooking liquid, lemon zest, and the remaining 1 tablespoon of olive

oil. Season to taste with salt and pepper. Add the mackerel and mix well.

5. Garnish with a heavy sprinkling of breadcrumbs and serve immediately.

Nutritional Facts (232 g per serving)

- Calories 470
- Fats 38 g
- Carbs 47 g
- Protein 35 g
- Sodium 278 mg

Salad of Salmon Teriyaki with Barley and Kale

Servings: 4

Ingredients

4 fillets of salmon

5 tbsp of soy sauce

1 tablespoon grated fresh ginger

three tbsp honey

½ cup rye

Water

5 cups stem, kale, and ribs Remove and roughly cut

Preparation

1. In a large mixing basin, combine the soy sauce, ginger, and honey to prepare the teriyaki marinade.

Allow the salmon to remain in the sauce for 30 minutes after coating it on both sides with the marinade.

2. In the meanwhile, heat a kettle of water to a boil. Add the barley to the boiling water and cook for 15 minutes, or until soft. Add the kale to the saucepan in the final 5 minutes of cooking time. Drain the water and put aside the barley/kale combination.

3. Melt the butter in a large pan over medium heat. Pour the remaining marinade into the pan and place the salmon skin side down. Cook for 10–15 minutes, rotating halfway through to ensure that both sides are well covered in the marinade.

4. Toss the heated salmon with greens and barley.

Nutritional Information (478 g per serving)

- Calories 720
- Fats 26 g
- Carbs 35 g
- Protein 84 g
- Sodium 1283 mg

Scallops with Quinoa Spicy and Kale

Servings: 4

Ingredients

2 tbsp extra-virgin olive oil (divided)

1 medium finely sliced shallot

½ teaspoons cumin powder

1 cup washed quinoa

¾ teaspoon harissa

2 cups chicken stock (low sodium)

2 cups lacinato kale, stems and ribs removed, leaves sliced

2 tbsp of lemon juice

Season with salt and pepper to taste.

Scallops, one pound

½ cup shelled and toasted pistachios

½ cup cilantro, finely chopped

Preparation

1. In a large skillet over medium-high heat, heat a tablespoon of oil. Sauté the shallot and cumin for approximately a minute, or until softened.

2. Combine the quinoa and harissa in a large mixing bowl.

3. Pour in the stock and bring it to a boil. Reduce the heat to medium and continue to cook, uncovered, for

15 minutes, or until the majority of the liquid has been absorbed.

4. Cover the saucepan with a lid and add the greens. Remove from the fire and continue to steam for 5-7 minutes, or until the kale has wilted. Season the quinoa with salt and pepper after squeezing the lemon juice over it. Toss all of the ingredients together with a fork. Serve the quinoa and greens on separate plates.

5. Heat the remaining oil in the same skillet over medium-high heat. Season the scallops with salt and pepper after drying them with paper towels. Fry the scallops for 3 minutes, or until golden brown. Cook for another minute on the other side after flipping.

6. Place the scallops on top of the quinoa and sprinkle with pistachios and cilantro.

Nutritional Information (320 g per serving)

- Calories 400
- Fats 17 g
- Carbs 38 g
- Protein 24 g
- Sodium 896 mg

Kale and prawn Madras Curry

Servings: 4

Ingredients

1 teaspoon oil

1 chopped onion

2 cups halved mushrooms

5 teaspoons store-bought Madras curry paste (use 1–2 teaspoons for a milder curry)

⅔ cup of water

1 can chopped tomatoes (14 oz.)

1 can chickpeas (14 oz.) drained and rinsed

3 cups kale, trimmed stems, and ribs leave coarsely chopped

1 cup uncooked, shelled, deveined tiger prawns

rice that has been cooked

Preparation

1. Heat the oil in a large skillet over medium heat. Cook until the onions are transparent, approximately 4 minutes. Cook for approximately 4 minutes, or until the liquid is released, after adding the mushrooms.

2. Cook until the curry paste is aromatic, approximately 2–3 minutes.

Bring the water, tomatoes, and chickpeas to a boil in a separate pot.

Allow it to simmer on low heat for 15 minutes, covered.

3. Add the kale and continue to cook for 5 minutes, covered.

4. Serve right away with prepared rice.

Nutritional Information (355 g per serving)

- Calories 406
- Fats 20 g
- Carbs 28 g
- Protein 26 g
- Sodium 1382 mg

Japanese-style Kale and cod

Servings: 4

Ingredients

2 tbsp. sesame oil, split

2 minced garlic cloves

1 tablespoon grated ginger

1 pound Tuscan kale, trimmed stems, and ribs leave coarsely chopped

½ c. rice wine

4 fillets of cod

2 tbsp of soy sauce

1 tablespoon toasted sesame seeds

Preparation

1. 1 tablespoon sesame oil, heated in a large pan over medium heat. Sauté the garlic and ginger for 30 seconds, or until fragrant. Toss in the greens with the aromatics. Pour in the rice wine and heat, covered, for 5 minutes, or until the kale is slightly wilted.

2. Take off the cover. Arrange the greens on top of the fish fillets.

Drizzle the fish with the remaining sesame oil and soy sauce.

Cover and heat for another 5-8 minutes, or until the salmon is cooked through.

3. Garnish the fish and greens with a liberal sprinkling of sesame seeds.

Nutritional Information (364 g per serving)

- Calories 325
- Fats 4 g
- Carbs 12 g
- Protein 47 g
- Sodium 608 mg

Recipes for Vegetarians

Pizza with Kale and Onions

Servings: 3 pizzas

Ingredients

Dough:

2 cups regular flour

2 cups all-purpose flour

1 ½ teaspoon of sea salt

1 teaspoon dry instant yeast

1 tablespoon extra virgin olive oil

1 ½ cups warm water

Toppings should be distributed evenly throughout the pizzas:

three tbsp olive oil

3 big finely sliced onions

3 garlic cloves, slivered

3 cups curly kale leaves, packed

3–4 ½ cups shredded cheddar

seasoned with salt and black pepper

3 tbsp olive oil for drizzling (optional)

Preparation

1. Whisk together the flour, salt, and yeast in a large mixing basin.

While combining the ingredients, drizzle in the oil and warm water. Continue kneading the dough for 5 minutes, or until it is smooth and easily comes off the edges of the basin. Drizzle some oil into the basin and coat the dough gently with it. Cover the bowl with a tea towel and let it aside for approximately an hour to proof.

2. Preheat the oven to 425 degrees Fahrenheit.

3. Heat the oil in a pan over medium heat for the topping.

Fry the onions for approximately 10 minutes, or until softened and golden brown. Cook until the kale has wilted, approximately 5 minutes, with the garlic. Season with salt and pepper to taste.

4. Flatten the dough. Place it on a lightly floured board and divide it into three equal portions. Each section should be rolled out as thinly as possible.

5. Place each pizza crust on a cookie sheet sprinkled with semolina flour. Top with greens and cheese on each. If desired, drizzle olive oil over the pizzas. 10-12 minutes in the oven. Serve immediately.

Nutritional Information (350 g per serving)

- Calories 1300
- Fats 69 g
- Carbs 139 g
- Protein 30 g
- Sodium 1417 mg

Curry with kale, chickpeas, and sweet potatoes

Servings: 4

Ingredients

3 tbsp extra-virgin olive oil (divided)

1 chopped onion 2 pounds sweet potato peeled and sliced into ½-inch chunks

5 minced garlic cloves

2 teaspoons grated fresh ginger

1 tsp. curry powder

2 lbs kale leaves

1 cup veggie broth

1 can (14 oz.) full-fat coconut milk

1 can chickpeas (14 oz.)

1 teaspoon lime juice

Season with salt and pepper to taste.

rice that has been freshly cooked

Preparation

1. Heat 2 tablespoons of oil in a large, deep pan over medium heat. Cook for 5 minutes, or until the onions are softened. Cook until the sweet potatoes are gently browned on both sides, approximately 5 minutes. Place the sweet potatoes in a clean basin.

2. Heat the remaining oil in the same skillet over medium-high heat. Fry the garlic, ginger, and curry powder for 30 seconds, or until aromatic. Cook for 1 minute after adding the kale.

Pour in the broth and the coconut milk (10 ounces (1 ¼ cup).

Cover the saucepan and reduce the heat to medium-low. Cook for 12-15 minutes, or until the kale has wilted. Add the sweet potato mixture and simmer, covered, for another 15 minutes, or until all of the veggies are soft.

3. Turn the heat up to medium-high. Simmer for 2-5 minutes, uncovered, to thicken the curry.

4. Turn off the heat in the skillet. Pour in the rest of the coconut milk and lime juice. Season with salt and pepper to taste.

5. Serve the curry over a dish of heated rice.

Nutritional Information (738 g per serving)

- Calories 879
- Fats 56 g
- Carbs 88 g
- Protein 21 g
- Sodium 524 mg

Baked Kale and Pumpkin Seed Risotto

Servings: 2

Ingredients

2 tbsp of olive oil

2 thinly chopped tiny onions

6 oz. risotto rice

4 oz. white wine

Season with salt and pepper to taste.

1 pint warmed low-sodium vegetable stock

two tbsp pumpkin seeds

¼ pound sliced kale leaves

4 tbsp. low-fat soft cheese

2 tbsp Parmesan cheese, grated

Preparation

1. Preheat the oven to 375 degrees Fahrenheit.

2. Heat the oil in a big, deep skillet over medium heat. Cook for 5 minutes, or until the onions are softened. Stir the rice and onions together for approximately 30 seconds, or until the grains begin to turn transparent. Increase the heat to medium-high and gradually pour the wine into the rice. Before adding extra wine, make sure the rice has completely absorbed it.

Continue stirring throughout the procedure until all of the wine has been consumed.

3. Season with salt and pepper to taste. Fill the pan halfway with heated stock and bring it to a medium boil. Cook the risotto in the oven for another 12 minutes, covered.

4. Meanwhile, roast the pumpkin seeds in a small pan over medium heat until golden brown.

5. Take the skillet out of the oven. Combine the greens and soft cheese. Replace the cover and return to the oven for another 10 minutes, or until the rice is soft.

6. Top the rice with the Parmesan and pumpkin seeds. Serve immediately.

Nutritional Information (658 g per serving)

- Calories 927
- Fats 54 g
- Carbs 86 g
- Protein 20 g
- Sodium 1034 mg

Fried Broccoli and Kale with Eggs and Polenta

Servings: 2

Ingredients

½ pounds broccoli florets, diced

½ pounds of kale leaves

2 garlic cloves, sliced

1 lemon's zest

½ pound polenta instant

3 tbsp Parmesan cheese, grated

4 medium eggs, split 2 tablespoons extra-virgin olive oil

Preparation

1. Heat a pot of water to a rolling boil. Place the broccoli florets and kale in a strainer and pour boiling water over them to blanch. Drain the water and place them on a platter.

2. Heat a tablespoon of oil in a big skillet. Season the broccoli and greens with salt and pepper to taste.

Stir-fry the veggies for 4-5 minutes, or until tender.

Combine the garlic and lemon zest in a mixing bowl.

3. Prepare the polenta according to the package directions. Incorporate the Parmesan and 1 tablespoon of olive oil into the cooked polenta.

4. Bring a small saucepan of water to a simmer. To make a whirlpool, add 2 tablespoons of white vinegar and swirl well with a spoon. Poach one egg in the middle of the whirlpool for 3-4 minutes, or until the egg whites are set.

Using a slotted spoon, remove the eggs.

5. Divide the polenta between two basins to construct. Top each with broccoli, kale, and a poached egg.

Nutritional Information (494 g per serving)

- Calories 998
- Fats 54 g
- Carbs 108 g
- Protein 30 g
- Sodium 359 mg

Spaghetti with Tomatoes and Kale

Servings: 4

Ingredients

6 oz. spaghetti

2 tbsp of olive oil

1 medium finely sliced red onion

2 chopped garlic cloves

Season with salt and pepper to taste.

1-pound fresh kale leaves

2 quarts halved grape tomatoes

⅓ cup chopped roasted almonds

¼ cup grated Parmesan cheese

Preparation

1. Prepare the pasta according to the package directions. ¼ cup of the cooking water should be saved. Keep the spaghetti warm by returning it to the saucepan.

2. Heat the oil in a large skillet over medium-high heat. Cook until the onion softens, approximately 5 minutes. Season with salt and pepper after adding the garlic. Fry for one more minute.

3. Add the kale and simmer covered for 2-3 minutes before uncovering for another minute, or until tender. Toss in the tomatoes and stir-fry for a minute, or until they are tender and thoroughly combined. Add

the greens and tomatoes to the pasta in the saucepan.

4. Toss the pasta with the kale mixture, almonds, Parmesan, and saved pasta water until completely combined.

Nutritional Information (585 g per serving)

- Calories 2140
- Fats 213 g
- Carbs 51 g
- Protein 20 g
- Sodium 170 mg

Fried Shallots with Bok Choy and Kale Fried Rice

Servings: 4

Ingredients

4 sliced shallots

four tbsp vegetable oil

2 cups kale leaves, chopped

2 cups Bok choy, chopped

2 minced garlic cloves

1 bird's eye chili, coarsely chopped (seeds removed for a milder version)

3 cups cooked rice (preferable if prepared the night before)

1 tbsp. soy sauce

To taste, season with salt and white pepper.

Preparation

1. Heat the oil in a small saucepan over medium heat. Fry the shallots for 8 minutes, or until golden brown. Remove them from the oil with a slotted spoon and drain them on a dish lined with paper towels. Keep the oil aside.

2. Heat 1 tablespoon of shallot oil in a large pan over high heat. Cook for one minute, or until the kale and Bok choy are slightly wilted. Place the veggies in a clean basin.

3. Heat another tablespoon of oil in the same skillet. Fry the garlic and chiles for approximately 15 seconds, or until aromatic. Stir in the rice, breaking up any big clumps as you go. Season with soy sauce, salt, and pepper to taste.

4. Combine the rice, greens, and Bok choy in a mixing bowl. Serve right away with a heavy dusting of fried shallots.

Nutritional Information (224 g per serving)

- Calories 328
- Fats 14 g
- Carbs 46 g
- Protein 5 g
- Sodium 103 mg

Macaroni and Cheese with Kale Pesto

Serving: 8

Ingredients

2 lbs elbow macaroni

1-pound fresh kale leaves

⅓ pound unsalted butter

½ cup chopped yellow onion

¼ teaspoon cayenne pepper 14 teaspoon garlic, diced

¼ cup regular flour

4 cups warmed milk

2 teaspoon Dijon mustard

2 cups grated aged cheddar

2 cups of Gruyere

⅓ cup Parmesan cheese, grated

2 tbsp chopped fresh Italian parsley

Season with salt and pepper to taste.

Spray cooking oil

⅔ cup freshly made bread crumbs

2 tbsp. olive oil

Preparation

1. Preheat the oven to 350 degrees Fahrenheit.

2. Boil a big pot of salted water over high heat. Cook the pasta according to the package directions. Set it aside to drain.

3. Bring approximately 2 inches of water to a boil in the same pot. Cook for 5 minutes, or until the kale is soft. Allow it to cool for a few minutes before gently squeezing to remove any excess water. Set it aside after finely chopping it.

4. Melt the butter in the same saucepan over medium heat. 5 minutes later, the onion should be transparent. Cook for another minute after adding the garlic. Cook for 2 minutes after whisking in the cayenne pepper and flour. Drizzle in the heated milk slowly while continually stirring. Bring the mixture to a mild boil for approximately a minute, or until the sauce thickens and becomes smooth.

5. Take the sauce off the heat. In batches, whisk in both slices of cheese, ensuring sure that all of the

cheese has melted. Season with salt and pepper to taste. Stir in the greens and parsley.

6. Toss the spaghetti with the sauce and place it in a 9x13 casserole dish greased with cooking spray.

7. Combine the bread crumbs and olive oil in a small bowl.

On top of the spaghetti, sprinkle the bread crumbs.

Bake for 30 minutes, or until the mixture is bubbling.

Nutritional Information (333 g per serving)

- Calories 727
- Fats 39 g
- Carbs 62 g
- Protein 33 g
- Sodium 677 mg

Conclusion

We hope you liked trying some of these 50 ways to include kale into your diet. You can see by now that it is not difficult to make, and it is a diverse and healthy vegetable. You've probably found ways to include this superfood in your favourite meals. The more nutritious alternatives we can make and ways we can include these potent food friends into our meals, the better our health will be.